pal·in·dro·ma·ni·a!

(pal′in-drō-mā′nē-ə!) *n.* 1. excessive excitement
or enthusiasm inspired by an obsession with words or
phrases that read exactly the same forward and backward.
2. Jon Agee's most expansive and entertaining volume
of palindromes, featuring comic-strip stories, absurd
diagrams, and lengthy monologues. 3. a state of mind you
may find yourself in after reading this book.

JON AGEE'S
PALINDROMANIA!

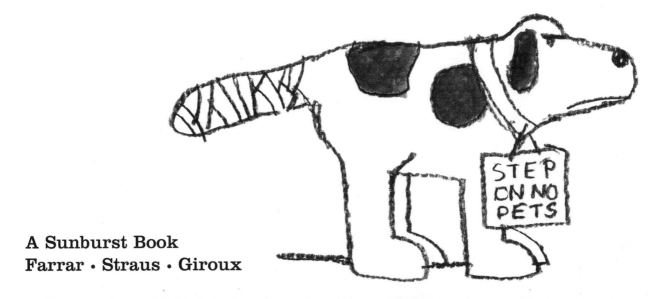

STEP
ON NO
PETS

A Sunburst Book
Farrar · Straus · Giroux

This book is dedicated to

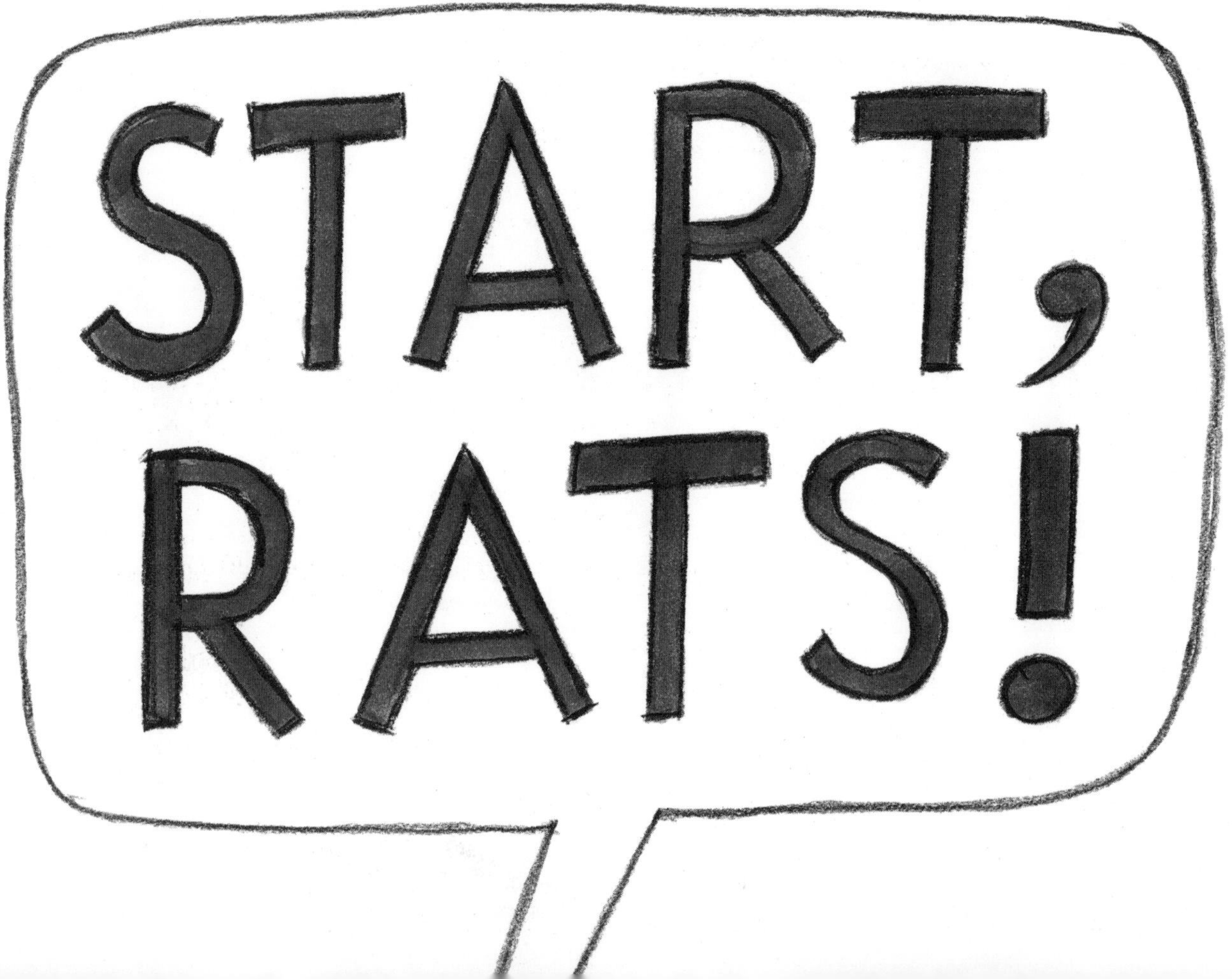
START, RATS!

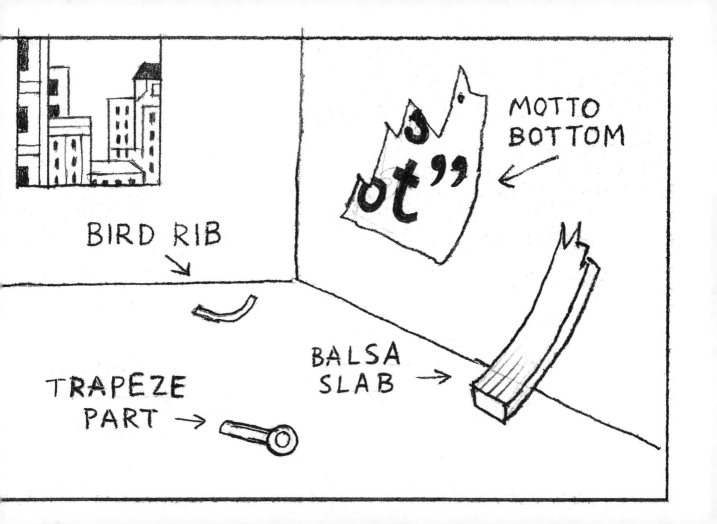

HOW PALINDROMES ARE
FORMED IN THE ATMOSPHERE

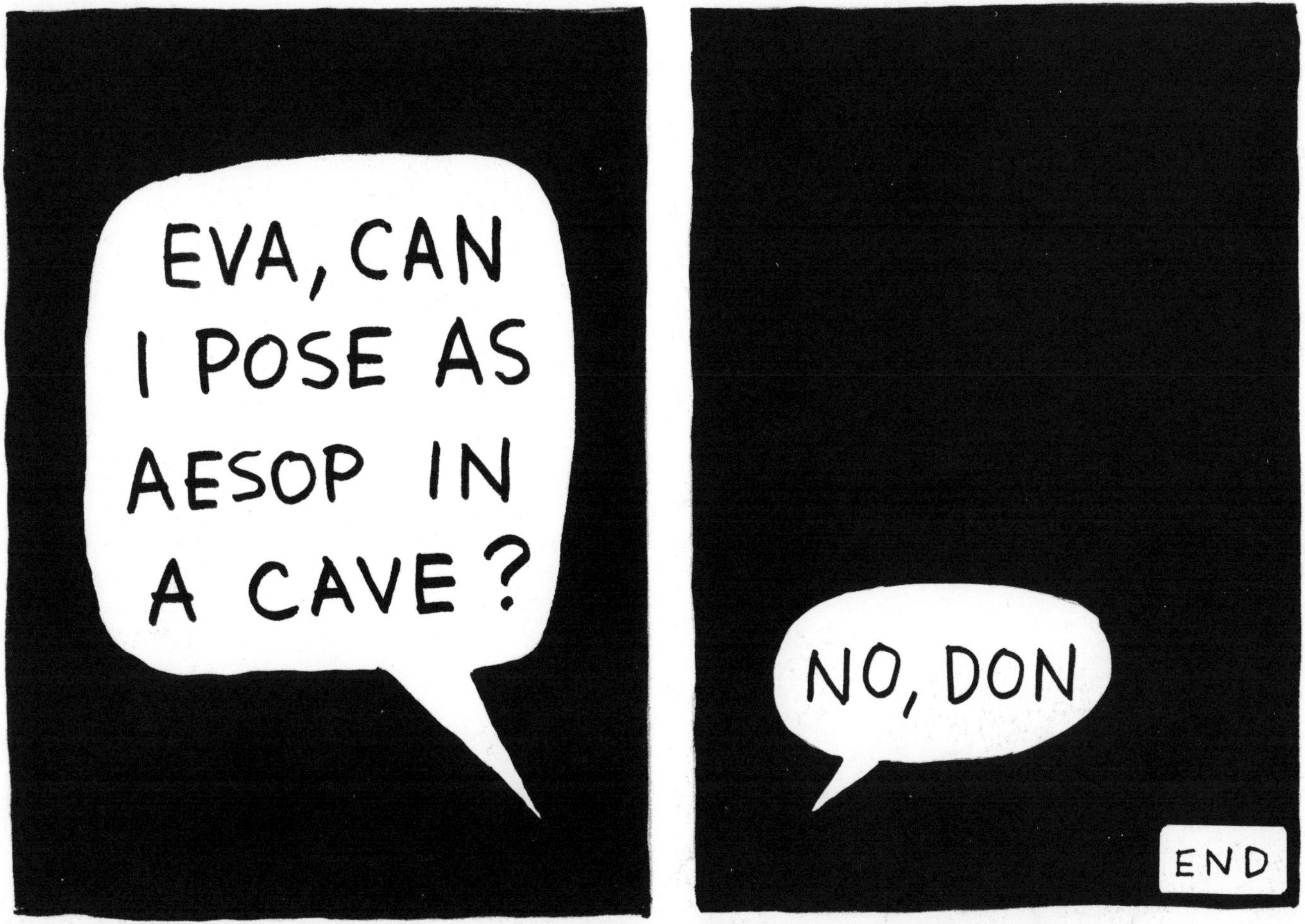
EVA, CAN I POSE AS AESOP IN A CAVE?
NO, DON
END

KRAMER'S REMARK

A NOVEL

MALAYALAM

FOR BEGINNERS

LE FALAFEL

101 NEW RECIPES

THE PALINDROMIC MIND

ROT! AN ESSENE GYM! PEE, KROENIG! AM I IN A CHASM? HARBOR? EH? HERO: BRAHMS...

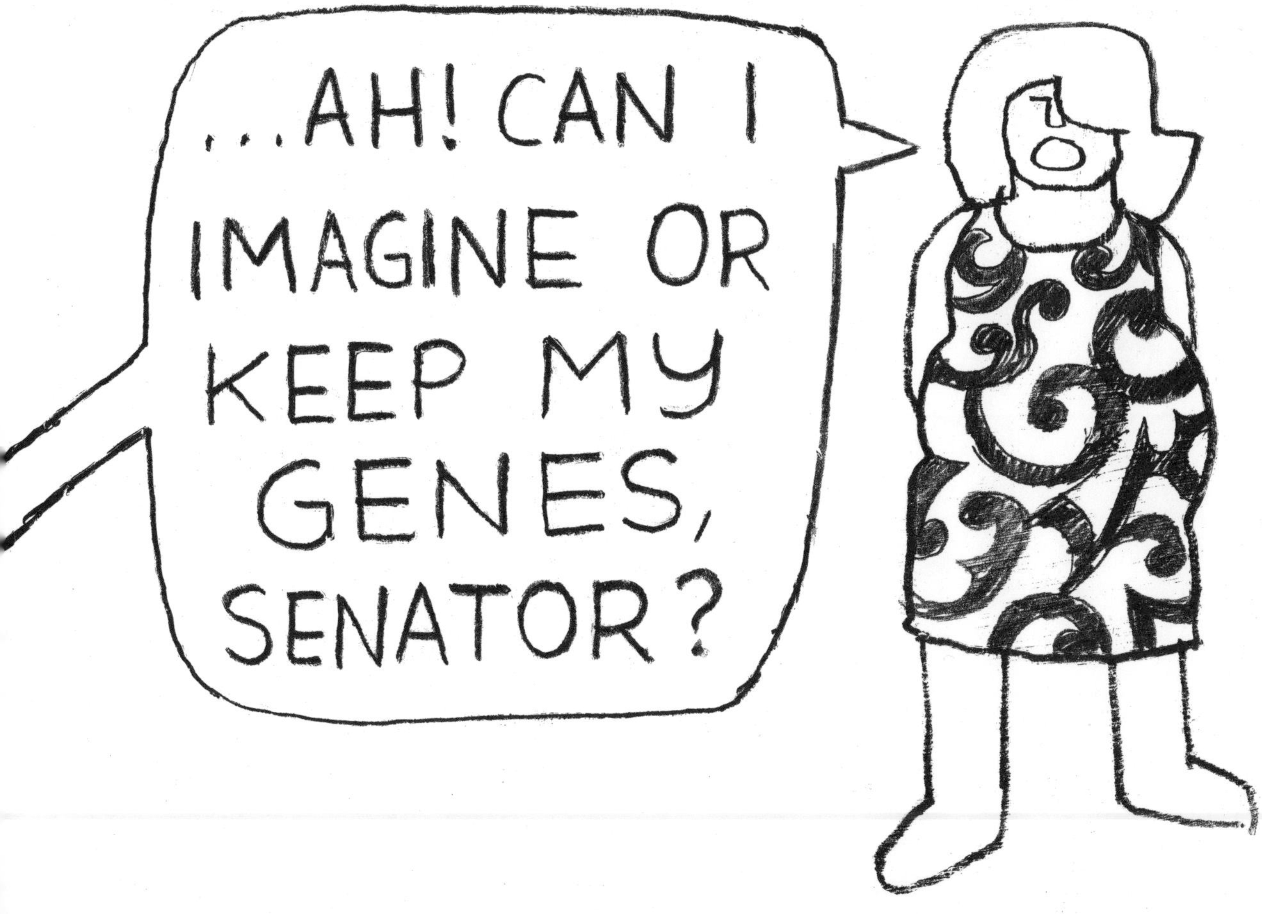
...AH! CAN I IMAGINE OR KEEP MY GENES, SENATOR?

A CAR, A MAN, A MARACA

A DOG, A PAN, A PAGODA

NED SAT IN ANITA'S DEN

BUT ANITA SAT IN A TUB

END

A TSAR, A NUN, A RASTA

A DAM, A RAT, A RAMADA

Monologue II

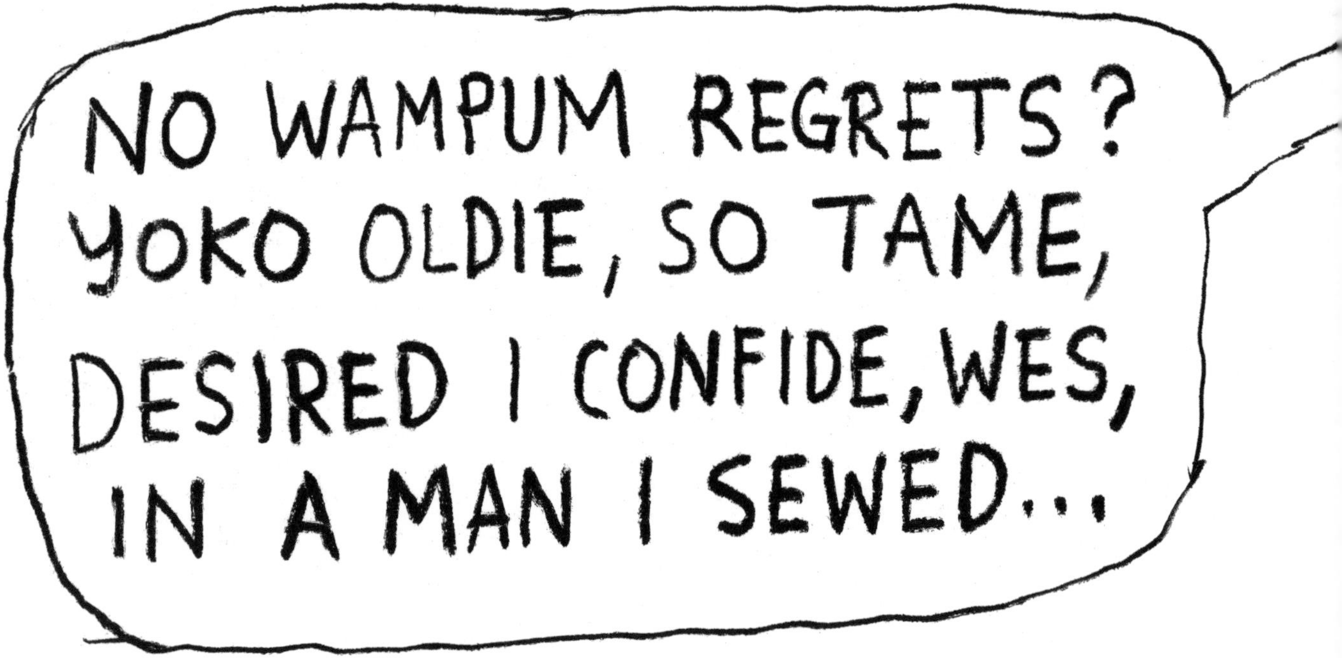

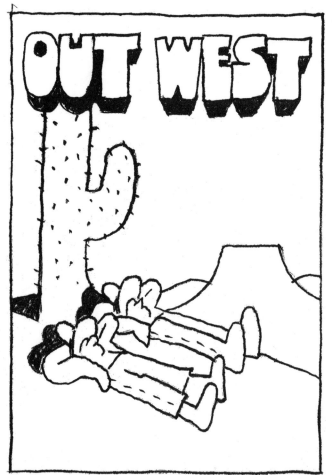

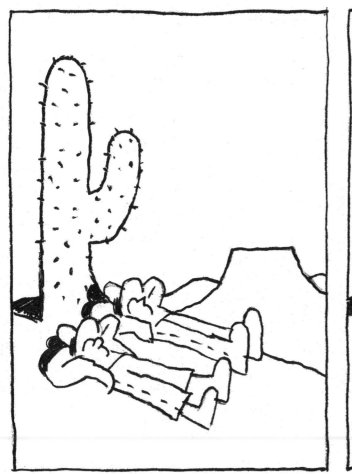

Acknowledgments

Of the approximately 170 palindromes in this book, almost half of them were arrived at independently by me. The others come from a variety of sources, including the following people: Dmitri Borgmann (EVA, CAN I STAB BATS IN A CAVE?); Russell Busch (SIX IS A SIX IS A SIX IS A . . .); Henry Campkin (DESSERTS I DESIRE NOT, SO LONG NO LOST ONE RISE DISTRESSED); G. R. Clarke (WAS IT A RAT I SAW?); John Connett ('TIS IN A DESOTO SEDAN I SIT!; WE PASSED ODESSA . . . PEW!); Emily Cox and Henry Rathvon (DO GEESE SEE GOD?); Dan Feigelson (LAST EGG GETS AL); Robert Gillespie (WONTON? NOT NOW); Yishane Lee (NATE BIT A TIBETAN); Leigh Mercer (WAS IT A CAR OR A CAT I SAW?; TOO BAD I HID A BOOT; SIT ON A POTATO PAN, OTIS!; SOME MEN INTERPRET NINE MEMOS); Dave Morice (ED, A FINAL PLAN. I FADE); and A. Cyril Pearson (RISE TO VOTE, SIR).

For "upside-down graffiti" I used names from a book called *Inversions*, by Scott Kim (New York: W. H. Freeman, 1989). I also referred to Michael Donner's *I Love Me, Vol. I* (Chapel Hill, N.C.: Algonquin Books, 1996) and O. V. Michaelsen's *Words at Play* (New York: Sterling Publishing, 1997). No book of palindromes would be complete without crediting Howard W. Bergerson's *Palindromes and Anagrams* (New York: Dover Press, 1973). Thanks to Will Shortz for the copy of *Herbst's Backward Dictionary* (an invaluable tool, along with a forward dictionary) and to Mark Saltveit, publisher of *The Palindromist*, for his research, advice, and enthusiasm. And to Phil Warton for drawing a couple of his original palindromes in my sketchbook twelve years ago, which got me hooked in a BIG way.

Apologies to Dan Allen for not using LAP TOP SYNOPSIS IS PONY'S POT PAL or DOG: ONE MAN, ONE GARAGE, NO NAME, NO GOD.

MALAYALAM is the name of a unidirectional language in southwestern India. EKALAKA LAKE exists in southern Montana. A DR. (Michael) AWKWARD also exists. He is the director of the Center for the Study of Black Literature and Culture at the University of Pennsylvania.

DeSoto, Evian, Honda, Isuzu, Kodak, Leica, MTV, Nikon, Popeye, Q-tips, Ramada, Spam, Subaru, Toyota, Tylenol, and Xanax are registered trademarks or brand names.

Library of Congress control number: 2002101771
Distributed in Canada by Douglas & McIntyre Ltd.
Printed in China
First edition, 2002
Sunburst edition, 2009
10 9 8 7 6 5 4 3 2 1

ISBN-13: 978-0-374-40025-5 (pbk.)
ISBN-10: 0-374-40025-3 (pbk.)